prey

prey

JEANANN VERLEE

Black
Lawrence
Press

Black
Lawrence
Press

www.blacklawrence.com

Executive Editor: Diane Goettel
Book and Cover Design: Amy Freels
Cover Art: "Prey" by Natalie Shau

Copyright © 2018 Jeanann Verlee
ISBN: 978-1-62557-802-0

Published 2018 by Black Lawrence Press.
Printed in the United States.

for Broken Thorn Sweet Blackberry

CONTENTS

"It's difficult to think yes. Or up.
When all you feel is fight or run."
—*Lidia Yuknavitch*

The Curse

When I arrive, fish rise belly-up
to the mouths of their tanks.

      Sewer rats gather at my feet,
      keel to their sides, stoic as stones.

Sparrows drop from trees in my wake,
spattering the sidewalk red.

      Above me, squirrels hang
      slack-necked from telephone wires.

Waterlogged mice float to the brim
of my rose oil tub, eyes bulging.

      Glass-eyed elk sprout from the walls
      of each restaurant I enter.

Pigeons and stray cats launch themselves
at my windows, leaving only a lonely smudge.

      All the neighborhood dogs
      turn up blue and foaming.

Yesterday, an elephant raged head-on
through my bedroom wall, bled out in my arms.

He Wants to Know Why Sometimes in the Face of Conflict I Neither Fight nor Flee, but Instead Go Disconcertingly Mute, Eyes Locked Ahead Like Some Sad Dead Thing Looking off into the Empty of Its Own Future

Children who have no escape
from the hands that harm
learn to die over and over again.

Ode to My Mother's Backhand

I loved, as a girl, to help paint your nails,
their perfect almond curve. Longed

for the same smooth knuckles, mimicked
the ritual of cream. I cannot forget the heavy,

honeyed scent you left behind. My elbows,
shoulders—the oily film remaining

after grab and shove. Effortlessly softening
the cruelty of any mood. O dainty left,

clattering with hand-me-down gold,
how I coveted your pitch, your reel.

The sharp bite of your angles. Sensuous
fingering of a cigarette, rocks glass.

Studied you, wrist-deep in the raw mash
of meat, egg, catsup, watered bread;

the whole-hand crush of canned tomatoes;
petite fork-whisk of powdered sugar into milk.

Eucalyptus rub on my congested chest,
your gentle swipe of tears, the intricate fold

and knotting of braids. How, I'm sure,
some part of me remembers your lift of breast

to my infant mouth, calm stroke of my hairless
scalp, the bath, the swaddling after.

Such precision, even in beer-battered rage,
to spin my jaw in whichever direction called.

The hot red blossoms you lured to my cheeks.
Shrill crash of a vase knocked from its shelf,

bowl of cereal struck from my hands.
The blood-tooth launched skyward.

O commander of attention, how I'd seize
at your slow rise from across a room.

Such power. A noiseless siren
wailing, *I will come for you, child.*

Secret Written from inside a Snake's Mouth*

In the mornings, when she was still,
overcome with quiet—less drunk than sober,
less fang than nurture, I would rise
before school an hour early, crawl into her bed,
nestle into her rising and sinking chest.
I'd lay there listening to the soft hum
of her warm breath, tuck myself under
her sleep-dead arm like something wanted.
Like a girl a mother could love.

---

* Venomous snakes immobilize prey by injecting a toxin which begins to
break down internal tissue, starting the digestion process before swallowing
the victim whole.

The Happy House

The house, they say, was once brick with a slate roof.
Changed in June after the new family moved in.

The morning after the last of the furniture was delivered,
all the leaves in the backyard dropped from the trees.

The warm red bricks frosted over, turned to solid ice.
Rosebushes in the front yellowed, then browned.

By July, pines along the block withered to brittle stalks.
Lawns and parks turned the color of wheat, the sky clouded.

Townsfolk took to down coats. Children returned to school.
Meteorologists puzzled. All the birds flew south.

A Good Life

They cornered the child in the forest.
Removed his clothes and loved him.
He walked home shirtless, stinking of men.
In high school, he kissed a girl.
Learned what to do with his tongue,
trained his fingers into fists.
He stole chocolate bars from the grocery,
lighter fluid, boxes of cigarettes.
Grew handsome and lean.
The first pregnant girl sent word
of her suicide in an unmarked envelope,
which he promptly burned.
The second made an easy wife.
He bought a simple house,
a lawnmower, two rusted cars.
Studied mythology and auto mechanics.
Took a job in a gas station
at the edge of a clumsy town.
High school girls gathered in the parking lot,
popping strawberry bubblegum,
eyeing the steady branches of his arms
as he wrenched and geared and oiled.
The dumpster behind the shop became a hamper
for undershorts smeared with pink lip gloss.
Caught fire every few weeks.
At home, he learned to wash plates
and fold towels. Take out the garbage,
bury hamsters, hammer nails into crooked things.
When the fourth child arrived, an idle boy
who smelled of mothballs,

he quit the auto shop. Took up chess. Cigars.
Pornography. The day the boy turned seven,
the man—now limp and grey as dishwater—
walked into the forest, found a blackbird to shoot.
When the bird refused to die,
he tore off its wing. It only looked at him
and blinked its stupid eye.
He delivered it to the river.
Watched its tiny beak fill with water.
Its eyes, gorge. He stroked its slick feathers,
their lovely, lovely gleam.

The Hunter, His Weapons

So many ways to take down a beast.
Smith & Wesson, Glock, bow, spear, Bowie knife.
Buck, antelope, bison, grizzly.
Duck, pheasant, quail. Bobcat, coyote.
The care he takes in preening:
dismantle, oil, polish, reassemble.
Displayed in an ornate case or above a mantle.
Assault rifle, sniper, bayonet, musket, six-shooter.
Hollow points and silver. Arrows dipped
in something shocking and murderous.
Sword, cutlass, machete, dagger, baton.
He is meticulous, gentle. *Buff, stroke, clean.*
Such dreadful worship.
More tenderness for the killing machine
than those who will die.
But when he discovers his hands
—those remarkable hammers—
his love is boundless, alarming. Unstoppable.
There she is, asleep at his side.
His knuckles buzzing, *Take, take.*

Unkind Years

Did he (drink to a stupor by noon / wither to bone / stash a case under the bed / drink it secret and warm / fling you against a wall / toss your goodbye pills / keep you from the knives / fuck you despite your unfortunate madness / play your song in the strip club / dance without you / silence you with silence / move to the couch / the floor / blame your wildness / blame your quick sickening / take the last of you on the living room hardwood / sharpen the blade before the cut / curse you) kiss you first?

The Sociopath's Wife Meets The Wheel of Death

Some don't watch.   I do.
I climb to the platform eager.
Spread myself against the wheel wide
as a starfish. Let him bind my wrists,
ankles. Wrap a pair of ruby lips
around the ball-gag.
Some stare at the spotlight
or into the dim of the crowd.
Prima donnas demand a blindfold of their own.
Not me.   I like to watch his eyes close,
watch as he tightens his mask.
Look,   how he stiffens
as the wheel begins its spin.
His free hand shaking beneath each knife.
With every reel-back, my muffled squeal
guides him toward the hit.
Each heavy *thunk* into the plank,
another moan. *Thunk! Mrmph. Thunk! Mrmph.*
Then, when the crowd least expects,
Thunk! Thunk! Thunk! Clockwork.
Gasps rise from the audience.
The wheel trembles.
I watch their faces, the horror.
Watch him steady for the finale,
his greedy dagger   hurling for my throat.

Secret Written from inside a Coyote's Mouth

I would sit a full lunch hour in the park waiting.[1]
Every day.
My shadow sagged her despicable shoulders.
Sunglasses hid my idiot eyes.
I skulked behind the pages of a book
as if my body could render so easily invisible.
There, I waited.
Predictable. Ordinary.
I waited days. Then weeks.
He did not come.
No, I didn't know what I was doing. Or, not doing.
Not exactly.
I only knew *escape* and its furious heat.
Each night, I'd arrive home,
rejection's dirty smear across my face.
A sin my husband could never kiss away.
Each night, I'd spice his soup with extra peppers.
More and more, each time.
Trying, however small, to burn us to the ground.[2]

---

[1] Coyotes are known for being devious.
[2] Coyotes are also known for being monogamous.

His Version

"I will not feel remorse for something I didn't do. I am not guilty for any of these crimes. I did not do anything of a sexual nature. I did not come on to any of these women."

—*from KFOR News Channel 4*

One Winter While Unemployed

He shows me a bustier made of shells, hand-stitched
in a country whose name mangles in my mouth.

This sure would look good on you, he gleams, shimmying
his body at mine. Something in my eyes silences him.

Oh right, your boyfriend, he retorts. And I don't say:
No, not because my boyfriend. Because you. You.

Not here. Not this. Not ever. Back away. Now. Not
dance. Not fever. Not laugh. Not skin. Not pucker.

Not scent. Not thigh. Not poem. Not linger. Not for all
the wine. Not for money. Not for soup. Not for rent.

Not bourbon or a smoke or a spot in a lit mag. Not you.
Not your well-traveled multi-lingual poems. Not this

cash-under-the-table, almost-a-job job. Not your library.
Not your files. Your sorted mail. Your dishes. Floors.

Prescriptions. Typos. Chatter. Not this bustier. Not
the next. Not after you wear me down. Not for threat.

For barter. Opportunity. Position. Not for champagne
brunch with literary elite. Book deal. Salary. Insurance.

I say nothing. I've cut him open with my eyes. He shifts
in place. Carefully returns the scant garment to its box,

recoils to another room. I return to shelving books.
One-by-one.   On my hands and knees.

Rearrangement Poem for the Mansplainer

"I'll chalk this up as yet another time that the white male privilege I happened to be born with makes me unable to speak my mind without being attacked. Again I meant no offense to anyone and was only trying to keep the discussion balanced. Be mindful of witch hunts, people. They can and do still happen. P.S. I can speak with truth and confidence here because I don't sexually assault people . . . just sayin'"
—unknown internet commenter

Chalk this up to being privileged.
Just as I attack truth to still the discussion.
My offenseS able me that.
I can speak, be, make, try, keep, here.
Hunt yet another witch.
Again, be mindful of people without
confidence, people sayin' no, stoP.
With time, I'll undo anyone, sexually speaking.
It can happen because I was born
with the means, male and white, balanced.
Only happened to assault _____
and _____
and _____
                    They don't mind.

Frat Boy

When I ripped her dress
(down to her waist),
her size D's flopping out
like the happy hands
of a birthday clown;
when my eyes locked there:
the perfect quarters of her areola,
the carnation-pink gumdrops
hard in the air-conditioned chill,
both flanked by tiny silver pearls;
when my mouth, which
(until that day)
had never offered her
a single word, spilled:
Damn, woman, I didn't know
your titties were pierced!
I waited.
But that stupid bitch
wouldn't even slap me.

Casanova Comes to Dinner (Or, the Poet and His Hundred Wives)

Your eye snags on the hook of an invincible smile. Handsome in his fedora and smooth smooth shimmer. He is full of bourbon and genius, and you just want one bite. And it's good, you think, to be the gal at his side, even once. And my, how smart you've become. How effortless, beautiful. Everyone wants a promise. You bring him home and he finds a sister to astonish. Visiting aunt, best friend, neighbor gal. Your mother. He pulls everyone into a different locked room. You finish preparing potatoes. Ignore the wall's thump, each unburdened moan. When everyone gathers at the table, someone comes crying. Someone loose on wine uses all the good curses. Someone lonely falls mute. Someone poised goes desperate. Dishes break, frames crash. The one with the most bruises shouts, *Back off, he's mine.*

The Summer of Supplemental Income

The foyer is ordinary Manhattan. Stark white everything,
   with chrome. Leather couch, ash-grey.

He appears from a back room, skin potent with sandalwood
   & labia. A loose kimono drapes him, barefoot.

Faux fur rug. MacBook squared to the edge of something
   minimalist & made of nickel. Flowerless, arid.

His hair sinks below his shoulders; wrists thin as rake
   handles. He is a jackhammer of good teeth.

I spot a girl exiting, twitchy as a runaway. She escapes beneath
   a mask of hair & hoodie. Scrambling. Like prey.

He's already nicknamed me *Gingergirl, Cutie Pie, Tiny-little-thing.*
   Studies my feet. Measures chest, waist, hip.

The room shrinks. His screen is an anatomy lesson: mouths
   collarbones ankles breasts thighs navels toes.

Even the runaway seems fifteen. I am twice that, but *clean*, he says,
   good genes. Offers to start lessons *today.*

Desperation is a cruel guardian. All the girls coughing up yeses.
   I imagine the massage table, smeared in oil & fluid.

Imagine the relief: Groceries.   Utilities.   Rent.

Commodity

In a humble, godless house
you moved through youth like any girl.
Dolls & other toys, yours,
      in parts.

You move through youth like any girl:
pink folds & acres of skin, pawned
      in parts.
Don't recall when your body became

pink folds & acres of skin. Pawned
toes, pelvic bone, pierced nipples.
Don't recall when your body became
not yours—just currency.

Your toes, pelvic bone, pierced nipples
featured on a fetish site. An agent's trinket.
Not yours—just currency:
oiled breasts, stiletto'd calves, shimmerlips.

Feature of the fetish sites, agent's trinket.
His doll & her toys (your
oiled breasts, stiletto'd calves, shimmerlips)
in his humble, godless house.

Question for the Boys Who Watched from the Window

Voyeurs / slack-jawed lemmings / watching slick boy / bad boy / sweet-
talker bully hustler Shawn / twist the cords / my wrists / his thumbs

    yanking clumsy panties to ankle / & all your countless
    eyes / giggles / hands smacking glass / like wild caged things /

rattling the whole goddamned house / I worried / the plaster would crack /
& your wire cutters / gutted window screen / rust & steel grazed

    your forearms / some, leaking a latticework of blood / then—
    the unbolted lock / & my small voice / coin jars snatched /

cabinet pilfered of its rum / mother's lingerie drawer / wormed through
by 16 grubby thumbs / still, your joy / still, now / 30 years / I see that joy

    in your faces / your eager eyes lapping up / my new skin /
    your new filth / to bury away / from future wives / & daughters /

& I want to know / what you kept / when recounting the story
in locker rooms / around campfires / over shots of whiskey

    & what you erased / our grocery money pocketed—for what? /
    cigarettes? the arcade? / some faceless woman's pink lace /

crusted under your pillows? / & that sweet, sweet rum / swilled
on the playground 'til you vomited? / such a good story, boys / such good

boys—
& I want to know / if you kept me / in the telling / did you

describe for them / my crumpled face / bramble of hair / each freckle /
my peach-colored cotton panties / flapping / dumb as a flag?

Pack Hunt

~~Count. 3 hours. 8 hands.~~
~~4 zippers. 2 breasts. 128 teeth.~~

Please don't hurt my dog.

~~Remember making love~~
~~to your husband here.~~

Please, just don't hurt my dog.

~~Swallow each joke. Each slap.~~
~~Every sour humiliation.~~

Ok. Just don't hurt my dog.

~~Curse the bourbon.~~
~~And your own gullibility.~~

No, please, don't hurt—

~~Consider escape. Race~~
~~for the stairs. Find a gun.~~

Please.

~~Beg for water. For mercy.~~
~~For morning.~~

Don't hurt my dog.

Secret Written from inside a Falcon's Mouth

I'm wearing whiskey's
        loose-fitted blouse,
                slamming shots & jokes,

& running mouth
        hard as the boys, louder
                even, & I shoot

my laughing mouth
        at a dare, & beneath it, shoot
                my whiplash hand—pounce[1]

in & down his pants,
        & they howl & applaud,
                & he does, too,

this brash & fast chick, me,
        a dare, perhaps, but the doing
                is mine, & laughter

balloons across the room,
        & we toast more shots
                under night's slick shame:

we claim men are cursed
        always with want, & so he laughs,
                & so I prey, his soft

& most delicate self
in my renegade hand.
His violation, all mine.

---

[1] pounce | /pouns/ | *verb*
• (of an animal or bird of prey) spring or swoop suddenly so as to catch prey.

His Version

"Lol. She couldn't even move. // She
was naked the whole time but she was,
like, dead. // Bitches is bitches. Fuck
'em. // I fingered her. // Delete that off
You-tube. Coach knows about it.
Seriously, delete it. // Her dad knows,
and if our names get brought up, she was
just really drunk. // You just gotta say
she was asleep. // Just say she passed
out. // Sir, this is Trent Mays. This is
all a misunderstanding. I just took care
of your daughter when she was drunk
and made sure she was safe. // Seriously,
I need as much help as I can get, bro. //
Did you take a video of me? // You
didn't take any pics or vids, did u? //
Spaz on her for me, bro, please. // She's
actin like I killed her or something. //
Yeah, she was so in love with me that
night."

—*from Mobile Broadcast News*

If We Were Meat

If we were the grey meat
    of boiled chickens

they would know better
    how to love us properly.

Would know it is best to suck
    the oil from their own lips

rather than try to parse it
    from the dead water.

Look, our bobbing girlheads
    in the pot. In the tub. The river.

All that hair and smudged lipstick.
    Is that a feather?

Look, all those gorged eyes.
    Imagine, all that sight.

Menace

"Have you ever taken a gun
out of the hands of a murderer

                                                 as a gift"

—Patrick Rosal

His hands were made of gears. His face, a cyclone. The jarring angles of his forearms, knuckles coiled around a Zippo. His eight-times-broken nose, crooked and whistling. The thud of his boot against the dog's haunches. Gaunt recess of his back, shirtless. Sweating. Knife's handle reaching skyward from the butt of his jeans.

★

They say I should've known it was coming.

★

He returned eleven times after his incarceration, despite the restraining order. He'd pilfer the yard, garage, cars, for tools of entry. Once, he scaled the bricks, climbed in through a kitchen window. Once, he stationed himself at the front door pressing his long, wiry index finger to the buzzer for hours, refusing to release. Once, rocks and spent beer cans at my bedroom window. It was discovering him at 3 a.m. on the porch wielding a hammer that stays with me. I still see his reflection behind me in shop windows. Still find his shadow lurking in my hallway mirror. His crumpled face, the low timbre of his voice.

★

I double-check every lock.

★

When he pressed the blade to my throat, detailed the exact sound of cutting through bone; when he said it was because he loved me, I dared him to try. *Do it, coward.* I grabbed his arm, *Do it.* Pressed harder, *Do it.* Then I waited. And waited. His face curled. His body lurched. I whispered, *You don't have it in you.* Then laughed with my whole terrified body. When he released the knife, stooped to the floor, sobbing, I considered the weapon. Considered his hunched back, the large roundness of it. Considered the blade's weight, size, sharpness. If it would sever a rib, empty a lung.

★

To write him into a monster means admitting I was a cutter, suicidal. A drunk. To write his truth, I must acknowledge my own. In the honest story, I have to tell you why he came for me. Why he returned again and again:

I was an orchard of forgiveness.

An orchestra of *yes* and *yes* and *yes*.
I unfurled my fists.
Softened every softness.

Invented new words for mercy.

The Most Dangerous Game

"Best sport in the world."
"For the hunter."
—Richard Connell

When he tells you about Joani, you cringe.
             Her dragging eyelids and thirst for bullets.
How she did it *in front of him.*

You come to understand his contempt for women.
             Appetite for skin.

Amanda full of pills. Nikki emptied at the wrist.
             Christa gassed in a Ford Explorer.

           //

Later, in the courtroom, you are asked to reenact:

           Hold the knife
           the way he held it.

Say the words
the way he spoke.

Years pass. He makes parole.
             Police suggest you move away.

Instead,
    you brush your hair, find your best dress.

Lock up the knives.
             Open each window.

Reprisal

she's in the kitchen, naked
save for the butcher's apron
streaked, you think, in wine

Secret Written from inside a Lion's Mouth

Most days, I stayed quiet as a hunted thing.
Shadowed. Full of worry.
I worried my own rabid hands.
Worried my feral mouth,
my hammering heart, its wildest.
I worried, too, his vodka-sharp tongue.
His unlatched wrath.
I worried, of course, for his joy, his honor.
Fears. Triumphs. Also, his rogue.
But I was rogue, too.
I worried myself mad.
Whispered through each day
cautious as a skittery hooved creature.
Scrubbed. Mended. Served his meals. Nodded.
In this way, we had peace.
I worried most that the worry[1] would be what finally
did us in. Its slow flame. Us, a tinderbox.

---

[1] "The lion and the calf shall lie down together but the calf won't get much sleep." (Woody Allen, "The Scrolls," *The New Republic*, 1974.)

The Sociopath's Wife Knows Endurance

What you don't know about the show—
after he dresses in his fineries, after the cape and top hat
(and you know it is I who straightened his bowtie),
after he sharpens the saw, after he smiles his broad teeth,
after he seals the box
(and you know I have already climbed inside),
after the saw parses my feet from ankles,
legs from knees, torso from hips
(and you know I should be screaming),
after my head is severed, heavy and mute
(and you know it is real because you saw the rigor of his arms,
watched him struggle against bone's cruel resistance
and the tricky catch of muscle),
after my body has leaked itself a flood
(and you know it must because you yourself
have before pricked a finger),
after he wipes clean the blade, after he unlatches the box
(and you know he must because it is his need
to show the world what he has done),
after he opens the lid
(and you know I will be gone, thin as hot red
seeped through the box's seams),
after you gasp your expected gasp and see
with your own eyes the box empty as a lie—
what you don't know is the massacre:
Sitting alone in my dressing room,
my drenched-red gown dusting the floor,
head in my lap, and how I begin: each slick limb
in my tender hands, I repeat over and over
every careful stitch: arm to elbow, torso to hip,

thigh to knee, ankle to foot, and, eventually,
with the mirror's grace, head to neck.
I build myself again stitch by stitch,
praising my hands—and too, his mercy,
always leaving my useful fingers: a way to endure.

Secret Written from inside a Vulture's Mouth

I stayed[1]

      for the children

                who never came[2].

---

[1] Vultures use their keen sense of smell to find freshly killed carrion and can strip a carcass in just a few hours.
[2] Vultures have the lowest reproduction rates of any bird, laying eggs as infrequently as every one or two years.

How Women Begot the Bible

She sits quiet, drunk on her own anger
    again & his despicable

drips down each fang just like
    the bourbon from out his pores—

don't misunderstand, she's seasoned, racked up
    husbands & guzzlers, & all she learned

from Mother who was no princess &
    all the grandmothers dating back

to the Revolution & perhaps even back
    to Babylon, too, the kind of ladies

whose mouths keep ready at the draw
    & even—sometimes—a knife

in the boot or under the cuff but always
    (all ways) a foot out the door

& no time for red ribbons in their hair
    or the tipped-hat gallantry of sailors &

cowboys, no, just a girl & her horse,
    perhaps, or her pen or her knuckles

or her two good feet, & today he's chiding her
    again & she knows someday soon—

not tomorrow, but one day—that sleeping quake
    in her will erupt & the whole house

will be on fire & she'll be gone so quick
    he'll wonder if she was ever real, maybe

just a night vision or a made-up thing
    like a Jackalope or Medusa or God.

Velocity

He tells you he would kill you
and you think of the early boys
you kissed at recess on playgrounds
and ball courts. Imagine them now,

rough bodies grown lean; studied
at the choke, pin, and meat of girls.
Hands, stubborn and impossibly strong;

mouths sharp as scorpions. At least one,
probably, a bona fide rapist and the others,
masters in the sport of taming women
too wild for caging. You taste them

in the bars after work, air thick
with testosterone, whistle, guffaw.
The bellow of each voice hammering

a waitress into flushed bustle and unease.
Smell their brawn under work shirts
and loose-laced boots. Their eyes
shrink-wrap you small; leers, potent

enough to unfasten a dress. They
crack their lips to show a slice of teeth,
offer a calculated nod. You sink

into a beer and beg a new god to vanish
you. Quell the spear of your tongue
lest it ignite the waiting landmine
of their brotherhood. You know

what it is to be hurled sticky-backed
to a barroom floor, men's room stall,
musty flatbed of a diesel truck.

Most of your years spent reckless
as a speedway, full of Southern Comfort
and colorful pills. You are no stranger
to feral heat, the pull of a shotgun, the holy

blaze of welt, cracked tooth, rug burn,
a row of tequila and salt. Carnal things.
Now you are forty and your teeth

are stained purple from wine. Those boys
who grew into men who grew into monsters
have forgotten your name. The only thing
left is to finish the bottle, smile and nod.

Secret Written from inside a Shark's Mouth

It wasn't all booze and inching toward death.
Love lived there, too.
It came sharp and vanished quick.[1]
One summer, he re-roofed the house
by himself. After hammering down
the felt underlayment, but
before starting the shingles,
he called for me to come admire his handiwork.
There, scrawled in bright white chalk
across the entire width of the roof:
"I ♡ YOU, JEANANN!"[2] and above it, him,
balancing on the high pitch, a beer in his fist,
broad grin spreading[3] across his sweat-streaked face.
Each piercing white letter now buried
beneath layers of slate for decades to come,[4]
reminding whomever next pries loose those shingles
exactly to whom I belong.

---

[1] Shark teeth are lost at a rate of at least one per week and can be replaced within a day of loss.

[2] Shark teeth are most frequently lost when they become stuck in prey and break or are forced out.

[3] Shark teeth nest in rows of 5–50, like a conveyor belt.

[4] Shark teeth fossilize after the remainder of the body has decomposed.

His Version

"It debilitates me to think that my actions have caused her emotional and physical stress . . . The thought of this is in my head every second of every day . . . These ideas never leave my mind. During the day, I shake uncontrollably from the amount I torment myself by thinking about what has happened . . . I've lost two jobs solely based on the reporting of my case . . . I've lost my chance to swim in the Olympics. I've lost my ability to obtain a Stanford degree, lost employment opportunity, my reputation, and most of all, my life."

—*from The Stanford Daily*

Secret Written from inside a Piranha's Mouth*†

He prefers winter. Prefers cabernet. Steak. Blondes. Prefers ass. Fake nails and glossy lips. Juicy. Stilettos. Prefers silence. And Comedy Central. IPAs. American football. Prefers bareback. Under 30. Commando. Prefers I know his preferences. Prefers not to be bothered with mine. Prefers I keep things quiet. Keep things to myself. Sinks his teeth and shreds. Prefers the spotlight be his alone. Dims the room and all the people in it. Prefers his teeth sharp. Prefers a little blood in his soup.

---

* Piranhas are omnivorous freshwater fish with powerful jaws and serrated teeth known to dilacerate prey.
† Piranhas practice cannibalism under extreme conditions.

The New Crucible

Act I   The Witches

We are women. It is enough.
We never boiled cats in a cauldron.
Never Greteled a girl in a stove.
No poisoned apples, no dancing nude in a forest.
Not even a song for the moon.
We have mistakes and privileges,
wounds, masks. We have thread and flour,
children. Perhaps a pair of red shoes.
Here again, the moon rises. And here again,
the preacher. And here again, the village.
We've been hunted before.
Dragged by our hair, mouthfuls of mud.
Salved burst lips and cigarette burns.
Been the blood at the stabbing, the break
in the bone. Here again, us.
Gossip rattling our doors, a hundred hungry dolls
in the cornfield, chanting our names.
Their torches lighting the sky.

Act II   The Preacher

I was your first murder, but you've forgotten.
Left your church after the rotted truth.
All the broken teeth.
Your stash of sucked-dry bones, the jars of hair.
You are running out of women to burn.
Stop blaming everyone else for your sins.

You snuck through the houses.
You slaughtered the dogs.
Now, your weeping, beguiled moppets.
Your devoted choir. They cannot unsing your crimes.
Face me, Parris. Come to my tombstone and pray.
Remember me. I was alive once.
I watched you pour the gasoline.
Mine was the voice begging *No*
when you struck the match.

Act III   The Village

When the man at the altar (microphone) speaks,
you say it is gospel. His word, The Word.
His hand on a good book (beer), his hand on his heart (penis).
If he says he did not murder, he did not murder.
If he says he did not lie, he did not lie.
And none shall speak against it.
And none shall speak at all.
And here again, the moon rises.
And here again, the preacher.
Oh, you gaggle of trained chickens,
you flurry of cluck and feather!
Let me drag you to the pile of charred bones.
Press your noses to the rotting flesh.
This woman was a teacher. This, a painter.
This girl, here, was a person. She had a heart and a face.
A mind of questions, ambitions, and love. She had love.
Look what you've done.
Your hands, covered in soot. The reek of smoke.
This mountain of bodies. This, your mother. Your sister.
Here, your own smoldering daughter.

Dumpster Full of Dresses

Wait for the second body. The third.
Wait and keep waiting. Severed fingers in the sink.
Blood in an old spaghetti sauce jar.
Shoes buried like bones throughout the yard.
Wait. Let the carcasses pile high as the house.
Let his lies grow families of their own.
Hush the girl against whose temple he holds the pistol.
Wait. Surely this time he will confess.

The Feast

Haul the carcasses through the basement
in double-layered garbage bags.
Leave a trail of Lysol spray to deter rats
and curious men. In the private hush
of the kitchen, unfold each broken girl
slowly. Praise each curved foot, every stiff
tiny hair behind the knees. Trace
their shoulder freckles, stroke forearms,
carefully detangle every thickness of their curls.

Retrieve the cleaver. Its thick handle left dusty
for years, unsuited to your vegetarian diet.
This will make him gleam. He will lay heaped
on the bed, smiling broad teeth. Listening
for each crack of breastplate, snap of femur.
When you open the skulls, he will giggle
a pitch so high, neighborhood dogs howl.

Prepare the delicacies. Pinkie fingers wrapped
in buttered braids of hair. De-boned toes
sautéed in garlic sage, like escargot. A rich stew
of blackened kidneys and milked liver. Ear lobes
dipped in the finest Swiss chocolate. Serve
the feast on trays of silver. Feed him by hand.
Slide each greasy morsel onto his fatted tongue.

When he is thick with bloat, present the final
course. From a gold-leafed bowl, a heap of plump,
raw, apple-sized hearts. Load his gaped mouth,
one-by-one. Wedge them deep into his throat

with your fist. Clog his gluttonous breath. Stand
above him as he writhes, his forehead beading
fat pearls of sweat. Skin, flushed a deepening
purple. His eyes choked in sweet hot terror.

For the Woman Who Loved the Predator More Than His Prey

"I wanted to write you a curse song."
—Marty McConnell

I would wish on you the knowing—knowing
with your own good body, but I am incapable.

You are made of flesh and nerve and thought,
of heart and love and wonder and grief, as I am.

Let me wish for you this: a deep sleep, trust
in the man at your back who has promised

sanctuary, and you have sipped of the sanctuary,
rolled your milk skin in it, leaned your eyelashes

on his breastplate, removed your bones for kindling
to warm his hands. And he has drunk of you and you

are almost whole in the clumsy wonder of maybe he
is the one, though he appears a strange divergence

from your girlhood imaginings (they say this
is always true). His mouth is filled with the world

and he is giving it all to you and you believe.
I will not wish for you the bruise.

The leap in the throat, shriek. The shock and scramble
in your own flowered sheets. His glazed eyes,

the sudden property you've become. You, a scatter
of dust beneath a heave of muscle. He culls your pleas

into a storm of thrust, grunt, drool. You, here, cannot move.
You are nothing more than your wit and your lungs

and neither seem enough. You are the torn cotton,
wrenched thigh, the perfect stone-colored fingerprints.

You are the scrub and the sob, all his countless
hands. I do not wish you become the night terrors.

The flashbacks. The grief and grief and grief.
Insomnia, delusion. The disbelief. The holy holy holy

holy holy wreck. The awe and burn. I do not wish you
stay. Stay and forgive. I do not wish you forgiveness.

Do not wish you cordial. Polite. I do not wish you his
manipulations, nor the mind's trickery. I will never

wish you "liar," as you have christened me.
I do not wish you answer *why* or *how* or *show me*

evidence. I do not wish you silence. Shame. Whiskey.
Box cutter. Xanax. Do not wish you erase. Erase.

I do not wish you anything to erase. I do not
wish you this. No. I will never wish you *this.*

Secret Written from inside a Crocodile's Mouth

Some take kickboxing classes or learn
to shoot firearms or move cities altogether.

I started wearing sports bras[1] to sleep.

---

[1] Reptiles of the Crocodilia order have an exoskeleton of bony scutes that serve as armor.

The Believer

He said *bruja* and she tended the kindling.
He said he could dance. She purchased new shoes.
Said pearl, she prepared oysters.
He said anchor, she bought a boat.
Said olive, she made of her arm a branch.
He said secret, she kept it.
Said hungry, she bought the bistro.
He said tequila, she gave him a grove of lime trees. The sea.
Said veal, she brought a field of pregnant cows.
He said loyal. She carved his name in her thigh.
Said open, she cut off her legs.
Said kiss, she mailed her lips.
He said that one. And that one, too.
She delivered pipe bombs to their stoops.
He said shank, she carried the gaping bodies.
He said she said, and though she never said it, she nodded.
He said, *Everything I've said to you is true.*
She knelt at his feet.
He said, *It is you who are the liar.*
She put a shotgun in her mouth.

The boy moving overseas asks to meet for coffee to address our "miscommunication" about his ongoing friendship with a man who raped me.

Go. Leave the apartment threadbare,
    stripped of its sheets & area rugs.

(Re)discover lands long colonized
    & all the sweet spice & pussy unearthed

(& colonized) by generations before you.
    Congratulations young wanderer.

Find whatever sunsets or forbidden
    indulgences might adorn your next poem.

Find love. Find a god. A backbone. Go.
    Learn a new preparation for lamb

with lemon & figs or an ancient word
    for coward. Go on, search for your soul

or some kind of forgiveness.
    This isn't riddance, dear boy.

            It's a burial.

The Unkindness

When she was rattled from the tree by an unspeakable boy,
the coven fell upon her, a din of schoolgirls.
Her feathers splayed in a hurricane across the sidewalk,
her *cheep cheep*ing gone on for days.
None knowing which bones to bind, what to feed.
No earthly idea how to teach flight.
They took her into the house, gave her a nest of tattered socks.
A lamp, a saucer of milk. They kept watch in shifts,
deterring snooping dogs and cruel brothers.

She learned to walk again. Perch upright,
eat hamburgers, speak a rusted English.
In time, the girls became no longer girls.
Her bones became their bones. Her chirp, their wildsong.
Their skin grew a coating of soft black down.
Each shoulder sprouted silvery plumes.
A network of new bones turned arms to wings, feet to talons.
Necks loosened. Each mouth birthed a hardened beak.
They took to gathering on the roof, flying circles in a ready row.

One afternoon, they spotted the bastard boy up to old tricks.
One hand up a girl's skirt, the other lighting her hair on fire.
The unkindness descended in a swarm.
He flapped and yelped, bellowed. Begged. Cried.
They swatted his face, pecked his cheeks.
Ravaged. Bloodied his eyes, removed his lips.
Scraped and hollowed. They ate and kept eating.

Alias

They tell me he's changing his name.
Dirty ol' beast.
While a woman slick with bruise
searches for a new city,
he's pulling on a fresh suit,
a good coat of paint.
Perhaps he'll cut his hair.
I am just the spoiled fish,
pungent and warm.
The gnawed apple core,
nameless body in the river.
On the street, schoolchildren
play with his beard.
Ask him for another joke, a cigarette.
He's everyone's best jester.
In his new skin, he'll be Brad or Karl.
Something reeking of toothpaste
and antibacterial soap.
He'll start with the smallest prey.
A girl made of lavender, perhaps.
Or one with a pair of scuffed shoes.
His is a body that has not had to survive.
It just keeps ticking, loud
as a whisper in church.
In his wake, a trail of carcasses
and spent condoms.
Sometimes, not even that.

Secret Written from inside a Grizzly's Mouth[*]

I adorn myself in wine

    because I am afraid

of me.

    The eye of my own tornado:

mouthshot and bucking.

    Skin coated in gunpowder

and teeth made of flint.

    Every few years I start a bonfire,

incinerate a mattress or a man

    or a city, then dust off the rubble

and rebegin from the nothing

    I built with my own hands.

---

[*] Originally named by American explorers Lewis and Clark, the Grizzly Bear was formally classified in 1815 by naturalist George Ord as *Ursus arctos horribilis* (brown bear + horrible), not for its grizzled fur but for its grisly character.

His Version

I honestly believe I was still asleep. Like, sleep walking. But Grade A Felony. I'm mortified. Humiliated. It's a sickness, you gotta believe me, there's a name for it. I looked it up on Google. I sleep and sometimes I do shit. I mean, when I was little I'd wake up in other parts of the house—ask my mom. I swear it wasn't intentional. I'm a good person. Oh god, I feel like a fucking monster. I know what she's been through, I am not like those people. Oh god. I said I didn't mean to, that I wouldn't do it again. Said I'd go to therapy and she—that night she fucking said she'd be okay and now it's all backwards. That's not fair. I mean, I don't think what I did could really cause "Post Traumatic Stress" but anyways, I've got a disorder, too. Why isn't anyone concerned about me? Besides, this was like, fucking years ago. I figured the whole thing would just blow over. Why can't she just fucking get over it?

—from Word Riot Magazine

Almighty

His twitch. His gaptooth. His meathook hands.
His whiskey. His cocaine. His lie.
His momma. His lie. His girl. His lie. His lie.
His mask. His blame. His finger-point.
His backstab. His *loyal*. His game.
His drunk. His spill. His fool. His freeload. His pass-out.
His breath. His dirt socks. His hole jeans. His unlaced laces.
His laundry but never a thank you. His *you-a-thorny-motherfucker*.
His train three hours for the dog. His guilt trip. His *you-owe-me-now*.
His joke. His charisma. His knotted fists.
His wrist-pin. His twice your size. His apology.
His *I'm-a-monster*. His *sleepwalk*. His *please-forgive-me*.
His *let's move on*. His wit. His shame. His slander. His secret blog.
His secret bigot. His *only for my boys on Long Island*.
His not job. His not tonight. His better things to do. His lies.
His curse the friends who don't cover his lies.
His beer bong and fried meat. His football and fried meat.
His don't call on Sunday, got football and girls and fried meat.
His stoned. His hostile. His high. His reel-back.
His snake tongue. His silver tooth. His rant. His bellow.
His heart. His *heart*. His saint.
His street corner kiss. His barroom kiss.
His always in front of a crowd kiss.
His never in front of his ex kiss. His win. His only when he wins.
His rant. His formula. His *legacy*. His fantasy.
His flair. His bathroom stall. His two-at-once. His brag.
His warrior. His broken. His moan. His *she-got-married*.
His *she-got-pregnant*. His lament. His commotion. His lie. His 6 a.m.
His derail. His marry me. His marry her. His marry her, too.
His *not-on-her-birthday*. His *we're-just-friends*. His *please-marry-me*.

His *I-can-give-you-children*. His *be-mine*. His *please please please*.
His not call you back. His pocketful of condoms.
His lies come out. His *let's-not-discuss-it*. His *details-don't-matter*.
His cordial. His victim. His martyr.
His won't stop texting. His won't stop emailing.
His wound. His mirage. His *bewildered*.
His *it's-been-six-fucking-months-get-over-it*. His threat. His dare.
His stalk. His grandeur. His monolith. His king. His omnipotent.
His everything. His lies. His everything. His *everything*.
His.

Poem in Which I Turn into Absence

smile
on the faceless body
                at the front desk

            limp sweater
        draped on the bar stool

nothing but hands
                for household chores

            blank page
where the resume should be

                    cache of sent emails
            to which no one responds

dog on the sidewalk
                dragging her leash

            wine glass sitting full
        on the counter

severed breasts
                waiting on his pillow

        row of empty shoes
leading
                to the fire escape

Secret Written from inside the Hunter's Mouth

When it was over—but before
he'd been chased out and rendered meaningless,
back when he would still peek
his face through windows
or arrive, unwelcome, everywhere;
the days when he
was still compelled
to send cruel letters
and describe for me in detail
the ways he intended to burn my body
or strip it of its skin;[1]
before the police rejected
the restraining order;[2]
before the last panic attack;
before the last suicide attempt,
but after the collapse
on the street in broad daylight
in a remote city—I replaced the rings
on my fingers with lead and steel: thicker,
sharper, infinitely heavier metals
to reinforce each precious bone,
and I practiced
swinging in the hot dark
of my empty apartment,
practiced on walls and doors
and lovers, practiced what it would be
to have his hands on me again,
or again, or again, *swing* and *left
hook* and *uppercut* and *jab*, I practiced

as though vigilance might be a thing at which
I could become expert, like prey
delusional enough to believe in a chance of escape.

---

[1] Excerpts from evidentiary documentation filed in QC SVB Police Report, Case No. 779, Sep. 2012: "immolate," "witches are for burning," "I know where you live," "shank," "scalp/scalper/scalpel," "better at being eaten," "I'll fucking bury you."

[2] Finding by Bureau Chief J. Flanders, DA for QC SVB, Case No. 779, Oct. 2012: "There is simply not enough evidence of threat to substantiate a restraining order."

Meditation on a Poem about Glass Embedded in the Scalp after a Car Accident

"You live through all of it, the impact,
The moment absorbed in the body"
—Luke Bauerlein

The poet writes about shards,
     how his body kept them, skin

grew over and eventually released
     the bits back into the world, something

foreign and useless, and I am
     familiar with the effect, having

picked the itchy glass of a Nissan
     from my own elbow as a child,

a full year after the Lincoln sped head-on
     into our lane, and it isn't very

different, or different at all,
     from how I wake at 3:06 a.m.

every day though it's been
     over three years and his shadow

still rides the length of my body
     as if it now belongs to me, how

my skin took in and grew over
    his violence and now spits it back

out in small fragments each time
    a man stands too close on the subway.

Madness in the Form of a Question

after Kimberly Grey

because your body still flinches, even beneath your husband
because the rise in your heart rate, whenever
because your body is a permanent record of all it has survived
because tattoos and wrist scars and toe nails grown too long
because it's only part of the story
because we are only part of the story, and we keep on
because a rush hour subway car is always a mine field
because you lost count of the times your body has been not-yours
because all the ways we take from each other
because the dolls are full of gossip
because they've got your name in their mouths
because they don't even bother to pronounce it
because the heat's out and the oven is all you've got
because the neighbor's radiator leaked down the wall
because rust and roach and lime stain
because persimmons
because mangoes
because meat is violent and so is the kiss
because nothing you say will ever un-make you
because the DA turned down the case
because you finally reported and the DA turned down the case
because you waited too long
because blame and blame and evidence
because the river
because the boy you loved as a girl is an urn of ash
because the lamp flickers and your hand reaches for a gun
because there is no gun
because your hands and sin and survive
because money is low and rent is due

because money is low
because an apartment is just another mouth to feed
because someone you love is always running out
because your mind is a kaleidoscope of ghosts
because your mind
because your body/mind/sin/flinch/heart/money/gun/wrist/name
because the story hurts worse each time you tell it

Hourglass in Service of the Sociopath's Wife

When the curtain opens, you see beneath the white hot spotlight:
    him, submerged in a glass chamber full of water.

He is bound in a straightjacket and wrapped in chains
    secured by brass locks. Beside the chamber,

an hourglass, its sand drifting downward, and me
    crowned in a peacock-feathered headdress and sequins.

I am fingering a ring of keys, wearing a mannequin's smile.
    This is what you have come to see. The spectacle. The dread.

If he escapes, what history! If he cannot—if the grains of sand
    run out, if I must drain the chamber and unlock his chains—

you will think him a fraud. And so you watch, jaw tight,
    hands clenched. He twists, wrestles, gently at first,

and you are confident in his practiced lungs, his dexterity,
    his cunning. Soon, however, his struggle grows and you glance

between me and the hourglass, calculating the appropriate level
    of concern. Still, I smile. The sand is quickening now

and I am smiling and he is thrashing against the water's weight.
    Gasps rise like applause through the crowd, your eyes dart

between my teeth and his whitening face. The sand runs dry
    and the keys spin aloof around my finger and still I smile.

He launches against the glass. And launches. And again. And then, stops. The water ripples and curls, slows to a halt.

The room weighs an ocean. The keys spin. The audience sits agape. My face, a betrayal of unbridled relief.

Beast // Never Been

I

stiletto girl / flip my hair & wink girl / lace & French manicure girl /
hand job for the Lobster Thermidor girl / cherries in my drink girl /
People Magazine girl / other cheek girl / hold my breath girl / suck in
my stomach girl / hold my hand girl / hold my hand cuz I'm scared girl
/ scared girl / scared of this mouth or this knuckle or this gun or death
or you or anything girl

II

   Anointed   deified   pampered   blessed

cherished   coddled   sanctified   hallowed

  forgiven.

      Never wanted that, anyhow.

III

to the moon or to the deep end of City Pool or to my mama's mama's
grave or to Lebanon or to Glasgow or to culinary arts school or to prison
or to the Guggenheim or to my first husband's funeral or to my mama's
funeral or to my rapists funerals or to my first love who tried to cut a gash
in my throat but instead I laughed in his face's funeral or to hell

IV
Boiled. De-beaked. Plucked. Skinned. Ground. Starved. Branded.
Hooked. Drowned. Electrified. Immolated. Gorged. Gagged.
Clubbed. Gassed. Bolted. Exsanguinated. Fried. Basted. Battered.

V
Buried.

ACKNOWLEDGEMENTS

Grateful acknowledgement to the editors of the following publications in which these poems first appeared, sometimes in earlier versions: *Artistica* ("The Feast" and "The Unkindness"); *Beech Street Review* ("Rearrangement Poem for the Mansplainer"); *(b)OINK* ("Beast // Never Been," "The Most Dangerous Game," and "Secret Written from inside a Piranha's Mouth"); *Bop Dead City* ("The Summer of Supplemental Income"); *BuzzFeed Reader* ("Ode to My Mother's Backhand"); *Cease, Cows* ("Casanova Comes to Dinner (Or, the Poet and His Hundred Wives)"); *The Dead Animal Handbook* ("The Curse"); *diode*: ("The Happy House," "Poem in Which I Turn into Absence," "Reprisal," "Secret Written from inside a Snake's Mouth," and "Secret Written from inside a Vulture's Mouth"); *FLAPPERHOUSE* ("How Women Begot the Bible"); *Foundry* ("Secret Written from inside a Crocodile's Mouth" and "Secret Written from inside a Shark's Mouth"); *FRiGG* ("The New Crucible" and "Menace"); *Hematopoiesis* ("He Wants to Know Why Sometimes in the Face of Conflict I Neither Fight nor Flee, but Instead Go Disconcertingly Mute, Eyes Locked Ahead Like Some Sad Dead Thing Looking off into the Empty of Its Own Future" and "Secret Written from inside the Hunter's Mouth"); *His Rib: Poems, Essays and Stories by HER* ("Pack Hunt"); *The Journal* ("Velocity"); *Milk Journal* ("Unkind Years"); *Muzzle Magazine* ("Meditation on a Poem about Glass Embedded in the Scalp after a Car Accident"); *NAILED Magazine* ("Alias," "For the Woman Who Loved the Predator More Than His Prey," "Hourglass in Service of the Sociopath's Wife," "Madness in the Form of a Question," "The Sociopath's Wife Knows Endurance," and "The Sociopath's Wife Meets The Wheel of Death"); *PANK Magazine* ("Almighty" and "Frat Boy"); *Polarity* ("A Good Life"); *Sugar House Review* ("Secret Written from inside a Coyote's Mouth," "Secret Written from inside a Falcon's Mouth," and "Secret Written from inside a Grizzly's Mouth"); *THRUSH Poetry Journal* ("Question for the Boys

Who Watched from the Window"); *Tinderbox* ("If We Were Meat"); *Vinyl* ("The boy moving overseas asks to meet for coffee to address our 'miscommunication' about his ongoing friendship with a man who raped me."); *Women's Studies Quarterly* ("Commodity" and "Secret Written from inside a Lion's Mouth"); *Word Riot* ("The Believer," "Dumpster Full of Dresses," and "His Version"); and *Yemassee* ("The Hunter, His Weapons" and "One Winter While Unemployed").

Further gratitude to the following individuals and organizations for recording and distribution of audio or video: Jeffrey Kay of the *speakeasynyc* YouTube channel ("Almighty"); Justin Woo and Wes Mongo Jolly of *IndieFeed: Performance Poetry* ("For the Woman Who Loved the Predator More Than His Prey"); and *Sound of Sugar: Sugar House Review Audio Blog* ("Secret Written from inside a Grizzly's Mouth").

NOTES

The epigraph for this collection is from *Chronology of Water* by Lidia Yuknavitch (Hawthorne Books, 2011).

This collection was named first runner-up for the 2016 Benjamin Saltman Poetry Award, selected by Aafa Weaver.

"Casanova Comes to Dinner (Or, the Poet and His Hundred Wives),"
"The Feast," and "The Summer of Supplemental Income" reappeared at *Drunk in a Midnight Choir.*

"Commodity" reappeared at *Split This Rock: The Quarry.*

"The Most Dangerous Game" borrows its title and epigraph from the short story by Richard Connell (*Collier's*, 1924).

The epigraph for "For the Woman Who Loved the Predator More Than His Prey" is from "Open Letter to the Straight Comedian Who Called Gay Domestic Violence 'A Fair Fucking Fight'" by Marty McConnell (*IndieFeed: Performance Poetry*, 2008).

"His Version" was deconstructed from the original singular persona to include excerpts of quotations from various interviews, news reports, and court documents. (Sources: 1. Daniel Holtzclaw (p. 17), "'I will not feel remorse for something I didn't do,' Former OKC police officer Daniel Holtzclaw talks about rape conviction," *KFOR News Channel 4*, May 21, 2016. 2. Trent Mays (p. 33), "Text Messages that led to convictions in the Steubenville Rape Trial," *Mobile Broadcast News*, March 17, 2013. 3. Brock Turner (p. 51), "Brock Turner's statement in trial and at his sentencing hearing," *The Stanford Daily*, June 10, 2016. 4. Author (p. 69), "His Version," *Word Riot*, November 15, 2012.)

"Meditation on a Poem about Glass Embedded in the Scalp after a Car Accident" was nominated by *Muzzle Magazine* for both Best of the Net and Bettering American Poetry and reappeared at The National Endowment for the Arts *Writers' Corner*. Its epigraph is from "What They Don't Tell You about Car Accidents" by Luke Bauerlein (*B O D Y Literary Journal*, 2014).

The epigraph for "Menace" is from "Boneshepherds' Lament" by Patrick Rosal (*Mascara Literary Review*, 2011, and *Boneshepherds*, Persea Books, 2011).

"The Unkindness" is so titled after the collective noun for ravens.

"Velocity" reappeared at *Soul Inscribed Hip Hop Poetics.*

The quotation offered by Eboni Hogan for the back cover is an excerpt from her poem, "15 Reasons Why Beer Is Better Than Women" (*Peaches & Buckshot,* by Eboni Hogan, mastered by Jason Marcus, 2010).

The quotation offered by Marty McConnell for the back cover is an excerpt from her poem, "lucky: for the last dude who asked why I'm so angry" (*EmilyRose* YouTube channel, 2012).

Select names and details in this collection have been altered for privacy.

GRATITUDE

This book and my survival are due in large part to Ian Khadan, Eboni Hogan, Missy Wahlers, Adam Falkner, and Jon Sands. And, too, The Unkindness, notably the women whose profound wisdoms grace this book's back cover.

This collection was conceived after designing a personalized gift in the same name for Catalina Ferro after rallying by Karen Grace. It is likely this book would not exist without them.

Indebted always to editors Jon Sands and Adam Falkner, whose critical eyes and difficult truths keep me ever-evolving. Grateful also to copy-editors Angela Leroux-Lindsey, Diane Goettel, and Rachel Kahan whose careful attention to the tiniest details make every difference.

"The New Crucible" and "The Unkindness" are dedicated to The Unkindness (AN, DC, DF, EH, GY, LP, MB, MF, MM, MN, RM, SM, TH, and TH). Infinite gratitude.

To the many individuals who chose to believe. And to stand.

To Scott Harris and Judy Davies for my being and my determination.

To Jon Deal for the journey home.

To Aulë who teaches me survival every day.

And to Callisto for keeping me kind.

Photo: Jonathan Saunders

Jeanann Verlee is a 2017 National Endowment for the Arts Poetry Fellow and the author of three books: *prey*, finalist for the Benjamin Saltman Award (Black Lawrence, 2018); *Said the Manic to the Muse* (Write Bloody, 2015); and *Racing Hummingbirds*, silver medal winner in the Independent Publisher Awards (Write Bloody, 2010). She is a recipient of the Third Coast Poetry Prize and the Sandy Crimmins National Prize, and her poems and essays appear in a number of journals, including *Adroit*, *BOAAT*, *BuzzFeed*, *VIDA*, and *Muzzle*. She has served as poetry editor for *Winter Tangerine Review* and *Union Station*, among others, and as copy editor for multiple individual collections. Verlee performs and facilitates workshops at schools, theatres, libraries, bookstores, and dive bars across North America. She collects tattoos, kisses Rottweilers, and believes in you. Find her at jeanannverlee.com.